GANDHI

First paperback printing 2007
First published in North America in 2005 by the
National Geographic Society
1145 17th Street N.W.
Washington, D.C. 20036-4688

Paperback ISBN: 978-1-4263-0132-2
Trade ISBN: 0-7922-3647-5
Library ISBN: 0-7922-3648-3
Library of Congress Cataloging-in-Publication Data available on request.

Originated in Hong Kong by Modern Age
Printed and bound in China by Midas Printing Limited

Design: Tall Tree
Cover design: Two Associates
Series editor: Miranda Smith
Editor: Paula Borton
Picture research: Caroline Wood

For Marshall Editions:
Publisher: Richard Green
Commissioning editor: Claudia Martin
Art director: Ivo Marloh
Picture manager: Veneta Bullen
Production: Anna Pauletti

For the National Geographic Society:
Director of Design and Illustrations:
Bea Jackson
Project editor: Priyanka Lamichhane

Consultant: Denis Judd is Professor of Imperial and Commonwealth History at London Metropolitan University, England.

Previous page: Mohandas Gandhi laughs with his two granddaughters, Ava and Manu, at Birla House in New Delhi.
Opposite: Gandhi plays with his grandson, Kanaa, during a walk on a beach in Bombay (now Mumbai).

GANDHI

THE YOUNG PROTESTER WHO FOUNDED A NATION

PHILIP WILKINSON

NATIONAL GEOGRAPHIC

WASHINGTON, D.C.

CONTENTS

EARLY YEARS

STUDENT AND LAWYER

RETURN TO INDIA

3

THE STRUGGLE FOR FREEDOM

4

EARLY YEARS

A Prime Minister's Son

On October 2, 1869, a baby boy was born in the city of Porbandar in western India. His name was Mohandas Karamchand Gandhi. When he was born, India was ruled by the British, but Gandhi would become a world-famous leader who steered his country toward independence.

British merchants first went to India to trade in the 17th century. They gradually took control of the whole country, which was rich in various resources. In 1858, the British appointed an official called a viceroy to rule India directly. Many other British people went to India to help run the country. But because India is so large the British relied a lot on the local Indian rulers. These princes were allowed some limited power in their own regions, but had to do what the viceroy told them. Each prince appointed an official called a *diwan*, or prime minister, to help him.

Ordinary Indians kept their traditional way of life and religions under British rule. The majority of Indians were Hindus, nearly 20 percent were Muslims, and the rest were followers of other faiths.

Previous page: The earliest known photograph of Gandhi was taken when he was seven years old.

Right: Gandhi's father, Karamchand, wears the elegant clothes of an official in western India.

1757
A great British military victory in Bengal, in northeastern India, establishes British rule over Bengal and beyond.

1857–1858
There is a mutiny in northern and central India. Soldiers and civilians unsuccessfully rebel against British rule.

Left: Mohandas (right), aged about 17, poses with his older brother Laxmidas. Laxmidas went on to practice law and became a government official.

But some Indian people were made much poorer under British rule.

Gandhi's father, Karamchand, was an important man. He was the diwan of the small city-state of Porbandar. He and his family were Hindus. Gandhi's mother, Putlibai, was Karamchand's fourth wife, and the young boy had many brothers and sisters. They all lived in a large house together with uncles, aunts, and cousins.

As well as Gandhi's father, his grandfather and uncle had served as diwans to various rulers in western India. His parents hoped that one of their sons would become a diwan too. Princes usually chose their diwans from families they knew well, so the Gandhi boys had a good chance.

Gandhi's parents knew that to become diwan he would have to work hard at school. He would also need to be able to deal with people, something he found hard because he was a shy, nervous child. When he was little, he was even afraid of ghosts.

The Hindu castes

Hindus in India were divided into four groups, or castes: *brahmans*, or priests; *kshatriyas*, or soldiers; *vaisyas*, or merchants; and *shudras*, or workers. Below the castes were the "untouchables," who were allowed to do only the worst jobs. People were born into their caste, and could not move from one to another. Gandhi's family belonged to the vaisya caste. But by Gandhi's time a vaisya did not have to be a merchant—he could do any job.

1858
Queen Victoria and the British government take over the rule of British India.

1862
The first child of Karamchand and Putlibai Gandhi, their daughter Raliatbehn, is born.

The Youngest Child

Mohandas Gandhi had a happy childhood. As the youngest boy in the family, he usually got his own way and often managed to escape punishment when he misbehaved. Because his parents were rich, he was not expected to work hard. Until he was seven years old, he had plenty of time to play and explore his home town.

In the late 19th century, most Indian children did not go to school. When they were old enough and strong enough, they had to start work. In many families, this meant that the girls helped their mother cook, clean the house, and look after the younger children. The boys would help their father in the fields or the workshop. Most families were so poor that this was the only way they could all earn enough money or grow enough food to survive.

Right: In this late 19th-century painting, bakers are shown rolling out cakes made of a grain called millet. Simple cakes such as these, served with or without other dishes, are still part of the staple diet of rich and poor alike in Gandhi's home region, Gujarat.

October 2, 1869
Mohandas Karamchand Gandhi is born. He is his parents' third and last son.

1870
Karamchand Gandhi becomes ruler of Porbandar when the local prince gives up his duties and turns to religion.

A brave act

Gandhi's mother was both brave and kind. When a scorpion came into the house and crawled onto her bare feet, she picked it up and dropped it out of the window, saving its life as well as her own.

Things were different in a rich household like the Gandhis'. Their children did not need to earn money, and there were plenty of servants to work around the house. So the young Gandhi children had plenty of time on their hands.

When he was small, Mohandas was known as Mohania, a shortened form of his name. He was able to play with all the other children in their large household. Everyone liked him, even though he looked rather odd, with his small, round head, thin neck, and ears that stuck out. He had a winning smile and was the special favorite of his mother and his sister Raliatbehn, who was seven years older than he was.

But Mohania was a quiet child who sometimes liked to get away from the bustle of the large family home where many relatives, visitors, and servants were always coming and going. He was happy on his own, scribbling patterns on the dirt floor or making models out of clay. He also liked to slip away, exploring the streets of Porbandar and watching people as they moved between the houses, temples, and the busy market.

Right: The market, with its displays of food and other items, was one of the busiest parts of an Indian town. Young Mohania was fascinated by the one in Porbandar.

Around 1874
Mohania enters a small local school in Porbandar.

Around 1875
Mohania and his friends are caught stealing from a local temple.

Above: Statues of Rama, one of the most popular of all the Hindu gods, are found both in temples and in small shrines in Indian homes.

One day, Mohania followed a religious procession to a temple on the edge of the town and spent all day there. When he returned, his mother was worried because she discovered he had eaten some flowers that she thought might be poisonous. She called a doctor who gave Mohania some medicine to take away the effects of the poison.

Mohania was friends with a small group of local children. They often played ball games, but Mohania was not very good at these. Sometimes he preferred to act as umpire. But he was always eager to take part in play-acting games. He and his friends copied the processions and ceremonies they saw in the Hindu temples in Porbandar. On one occasion, they thought it would be fun if they stole some of the statues from a temple to use in their games. Mohania and his friends crept into the temple while the priest was having his afternoon nap. But when one of them dropped a metal statue, it made a clattering noise on the hard, stone floor. The priest's wife heard them and raised the alarm. The children were caught, but the only one who admitted that he was guilty was Mohania. Even when he was six years old he preferred to tell the truth.

1876
Queen Victoria takes the title "Empress of India."

1876
Karamchand Gandhi is appointed diwan of Rajkot State.

A young prince

As a small boy, Mohania liked to travel around the countryside in a cart pulled by a young bull. Because he was the diwan's son, people used to treat him like a young prince, giving him presents of food or money.

By this time, Mohania was a pupil at a small local school. Many of the lessons were held out of doors, and the children practiced writing in the local Gujarati language by scraping letters in the dust with a stick. It all seemed very easy, and Mohania began to love his Gujarati language, as he would for the rest of his life.

Below: Mohania began his education at a simple local school like this, learning his letters before going on to the more formal primary school in Porbandar.

1877
There is a serious famine in Bengal in northeastern India.

1878
The Gandhi family moves to Rajkot to join Karamchand.

The Raj

By the late 19th century the whole of India was part of the British Empire, as shown on the map below. British India also covered the areas that are now Pakistan (Sind, Baluchistan, Punjab, and Northwest Frontier), Bangladesh (then East Bengal), and Myanmar. The British government of India was known as the Raj, which means "rule." British officials ran much of India directly. But in some parts of the country (shown in yellow) Indian leaders were allowed to keep power over their own areas, provided that they swore an oath of allegiance to Britain. India added hugely to British wealth. The British sent Indian raw materials such as cotton home to England, where they were made into goods that British traders sold back to the Indians.

Above: The British queen, Victoria, took the title of Empress of India in 1876, but she never visited the country. India was ruled on her behalf by a British official called a viceroy.

AFGHANISTAN

KASHMIR & JAMMU

NW FRONTIER

PUNJAB

Amritsar

BALUCHISTAN

RAJPUTANA

Delhi

NEPAL

BHUTAN

SIND

Champaran
Lucknow

KATHIAWAR Sabarmati

EAST BENGAL

Rajkot

Ahmedabad

Calcutta
(Kolkata)

Porbandar

Dandi

BRITISH INDIA

BURMA
(MYANMAR)

Gujarat

Bombay (Mumbai)

Poona

Arabian Sea

Bay of Bengal

Madras

N

W   E

S

Princely states

Ruled directly
by Britain

CEYLON
(SRI LANKA)

Indian Ocean

Right: Prince Albert was the son of the Maharaja Duleep Singh, who ruled part of northwestern India, the Punjab. After he lost his kingdom to the British, Duleep Singh and his family went to live in England.

Below: This group of British hunters in the 1920s includes the viceroy, Lord Reading (kneeling, left), and several Indian servants. The British liked tiger hunting: Their ability to bring down India's most beautiful animal seemed to symbolize their control of the country.

On the Move

While Mohania was learning his letters, his father found a new job, as diwan to the prince of the nearby town of Rajkot. So when Mohania was eight, the whole family moved. Their new home was a big house with high walls and shaded courtyards. For Mohania, the move also meant going to the Taluka Primary School at Rajkot.

At his new school, Mohania learned several new subjects, including math, history, and geography. In his first year, he lost many days of school because of illness—he and several other members of his family had a bad fever. But he did better in his second year, improving his marks in math even though he found it difficult to learn his tables. Although he did not find lessons in the new subjects easy, Mohania was eager to learn. He always tried to get to school on time and complained if his breakfast was late.

After two years of the primary school, Mohania took the entrance examination for high school.

Right: When Mohania's family moved to Rajkot, he was sent to this primary school. He was not a fast learner, and knew that the only way to do well would be to work hard.

1879
The British defeat the Zulus of the Natal region of South Africa.

1879
Mohania starts at the Taluka Primary School, Rajkot.

> *"I used to be very shy and avoided all company....*
> *To be at the school at the stroke of the hour and to run back*
> *home as soon as the school closed—that was my daily habit,*
> *because I could not bear to talk to anybody."*
>
> **Mohandas Gandhi, *M.K. Gandhi: An Autobiography*, 1927**

He did quite well, coming ninth out of the 69 who took the exam. He lost some points because his handwriting was messy.

When he started at the local Kathiawar High School, he did badly in many subjects. One problem was that the teachers spoke English, a language that Mohania found very hard. All the lessons—math, history, geography, and astronomy—were taught in English. At the end of his first year, Mohania failed English spelling. He was at the bottom of his class.

Mohania and his classmates wrote with chalk on small slates in class. One day, he was doing an English spelling test when a school inspector visited his class. The teacher saw that Mohania was having trouble with spelling the word "kettle." The teacher wanted to impress the inspector, so he made signs at Mohania to copy his neighbor's spelling. Mohania did not understand. When the incident was explained to him later, he said that he did not think it was right to copy someone else's work.

Ruler of Rajkot
Mohania's father's new job in Rajkot was as diwan with full powers. This meant that he ruled on behalf of the local prince, so he was the most powerful man in town.

1880
Mohania enters the Kathiawar High School, Rajkot.

1881
Mohania ranks at the bottom of his class in his first year at high school.

Child Marriage

One of the most important events in Mohania's life took place when he was 13. He got married to a girl named Kasturbai Makanji, who was also 13 years old. She was the daughter of a merchant who lived near his former family home in Porbandar. Child marriage was very common in India at this time. Young people were not allowed to choose a partner: The marriage was arranged by their parents.

Left: A traditional Hindu wedding ceremony takes place under a special decorated canopy called a *mandap*, which is normally set up at the bride's home. Here a veiled bride and groom, along with family members, have gathered beneath the mandap.

Hindu weddings are very splendid occasions, particularly when the families are wealthy. Both families make special clothes and jewelry, and there are costly presents and a big feast. This can be very expensive, so the Gandhis decided to have a triple wedding, marrying two other family members at the same time to save money. The ceremony went very well.

1882	1883
Mohania marries Kasturbai Makanji.	Mohania promises to work harder at school and is allowed to enter a higher grade.

Tied by a thread

At Hindu weddings a sacred thread is often wound around the couple's wrists or shoulders, tying the pair together. This is a symbol that the man and woman will spend the rest of their lives together.

The only upset was that Mohania's father had a fall on the way there and arrived covered in bandages.

The couple had a good time. They enjoyed the colorful clothes and rich food. After the wedding, they lived at home with Mohania's parents, but Kasturbai went back to Porbandar to live with her own parents for several months each year. Mohania and Kasturbai barely knew each other when they married, but Kasturbai proved to be a good partner for Mohania. She was strong-willed but caring, and the pair gradually came to love one another. Their marriage would last for 62 years.

Marriage meant that Mohania had to take more time off from his lessons. As well as spending time with his young bride, he was also caring for his father, who was ill after his fall. In the year he got married, he missed 148 days of school and did not even take the end-of-year exam. But the following year, he promised to work harder. Soon he was getting much better marks, especially in English and math, and rose to fourth in his class. His parents thought that he might become a diwan after all.

> *"I do not think it [marriage] meant anything more than the prospect of good clothes to wear, drum beating, marriage processions, rich dinners..."*
> **Mohandas Gandhi, *M.K. Gandhi: An Autobiography*, 1927**

1883
An Indian National Conference takes place to discuss the problems faced by the Indian people under British rule.

1884
Mohania's marks begin to improve.

Religion or Rebellion?

Like most teenagers, Mohania was tempted to reject the values of his parents. As Hindus, his family believed that eating meat and smoking were wrong. But India's British rulers, and India's Muslims, ate meat, so Mohania and some of his friends decided they should try it too.

Above: One of the heroes of the *Ramayana* is the monkey-god, Hanuman. In the poem, the demon Ravana kidnaps Sita, Rama's wife. Here, Hanuman is fighting Ravana's son, Indrajit, during the struggle to rescue Sita.

One of Mohania's friends was called Mehtab. Mehtab told Mohania that if he ate meat, he would grow big and brave. So Mohania tried a meat dish in secret with Mehtab, but he did not like the tough goat meat that he was given. Mohania soon gave up trying to eat meat.

When Mohania was 16, his father became seriously ill with an ulcer. Mohania spent a lot of time nursing him, but Karamchand finally died of his illness. For the rest of his life, Mohania felt deeply sorry he was not at his father's bedside when he died.

Mohania began to realize that the Hindu religion had something to teach him. He liked the stories of the Hindu gods and heroes, whose examples helped him see the importance of truth, courage, and duty.

1885
Gandhi's father, Karamchand, dies.

1885
The Indian National Congress movement is founded to discuss India's future in cooperation with the British.

He was fascinated by the peaceful courage of Lord Rama, whose adventures are told in a great epic poem, the *Ramayana*. Another hero was Harishchandra, a king who gave up everything he owned for the sake of truth.

Mohania continued studying hard at school, and passed his end-of-school examinations. Then he started college at Bhavnagar, about 90 miles from home. But he could not seem to concentrate on his studies and wondered what he could do with his life. A family friend suggested he go to England to study law: It would be perfect training to be a diwan back in India. He could not take Kasturbai and their baby son, Harilal, all the way to England, so they would have to stay at home.

Tall story

Some Indians believed that meat-eating made many British people five cubits (or six feet) tall. They even had a rhyme about this:

"Behold the mighty Englishman,
He rules the Indian small,
Because being a meat-eater,
He is five cubits tall."

Below: Rama, a god to whom Gandhi was especially devoted, relaxes with his wife, Sita, on the back of a water serpent.

1888
Gandhi enters college at Bhavnagar, but leaves at the end of his first term.

1888
Gandhi's first son, Harilal, is born.

STUDENT AND LAWYER

2

Studying Law

At first, Gandhi's mother did not want him to leave home. But she finally agreed, provided that he would promise not to drink alcohol or eat meat. So when he was 19, Gandhi made the seven-week boat trip to England.

When he arrived in London he enrolled at the Inner Temple, one of the Inns of Court where you could train to be a lawyer.

To begin with, Gandhi tried to turn himself into an "English gentleman." He bought himself a new suit and a top hat, and started to read the British newspapers to help improve his English. But he soon realized that living the life of a gentleman cost a lot of money. So he moved to an inexpensive room and began to walk everywhere instead of taking trains or taxis.

To become a lawyer, a trainee had to do two things: pass law examinations and "keep terms" (in other words, eat a set number of meals in the dining hall at his Inn of Court). Gandhi was popular at dinner: Since he did not drink alcohol, other diners could have his share of the wine.

Above: Gandhi joined the London Vegetarian Society. This group of men and women took him to vegetarian restaurants and loaned him books about vegetarian food. He wrote articles about Indian food for the magazine they produced.

Previous page: As a young man of 18, Gandhi began to dress in the kinds of clothes worn by professional people in Europe.

September 1888
Gandhi sets sail for England, leaving Kasturbai and Harilal at home.

November 1888
Gandhi enrolls at the Inner Temple, London, and begins to study law.

Gandhi's guidebook

Because Gandhi walked everywhere, he soon knew London very well. So he wrote a guidebook to the city, aimed especially at foreign students like himself who were trying to find their way around.

Studying for the law examinations was very difficult. Gandhi knew he had to work hard to improve his marks at school, so he made a big effort. He carefully read all the textbooks and studied Roman law in the original Latin. Most students did not work as hard as he did. They read simplified notes that gave them just the basics. But he wanted to be well-prepared.

On June 10, 1891, Gandhi passed his examinations. He was now qualified to work as a lawyer in Britain or anywhere in the British Empire. Two days later, he boarded a ship bound for his home country to begin his working life.

Below: These grand London buildings contain the Inner Temple Library, where Gandhi read about many past court cases.

1889
Gandhi begins his study of world religions.

1891
Gandhi passes his law examinations and returns to India.

Gandhi's Beliefs

Gandhi was brought up as a Hindu, but he did not begin to think very deeply about religion until he went to live in England. In London, he discovered that the Hindu scriptures, originally written in the ancient Sanskrit language, had been translated into English. He found that he could read them easily. Soon, he began to discover the writings of the other faiths of the world, and a number of his British friends encouraged him in his reading. Gandhi was also interested in a religion then little-known outside India—Jainism. The Jains rejected all violence toward living things, and this belief influenced Gandhi when he began to find ways of protesting about political issues without the use of force. Gandhi respected all the religions he read about and realized that it was important for all Indians to do the same. Too many of India's problems were caused by disagreements between the followers of different faiths.

Above: Sir Edwin Arnold was an important member of the Vegetarian Society when Gandhi met him in London. Arnold was an expert on world religions. He had translated some of the Hindu scriptures from the Sanskrit language.

Left: Gandhi's friend Annie Besant was a writer, socialist, and leader of a group called the Theosophists. The Theosophists tried to understand the ideas that were common to all religions. They valued all of the great religious teachers.

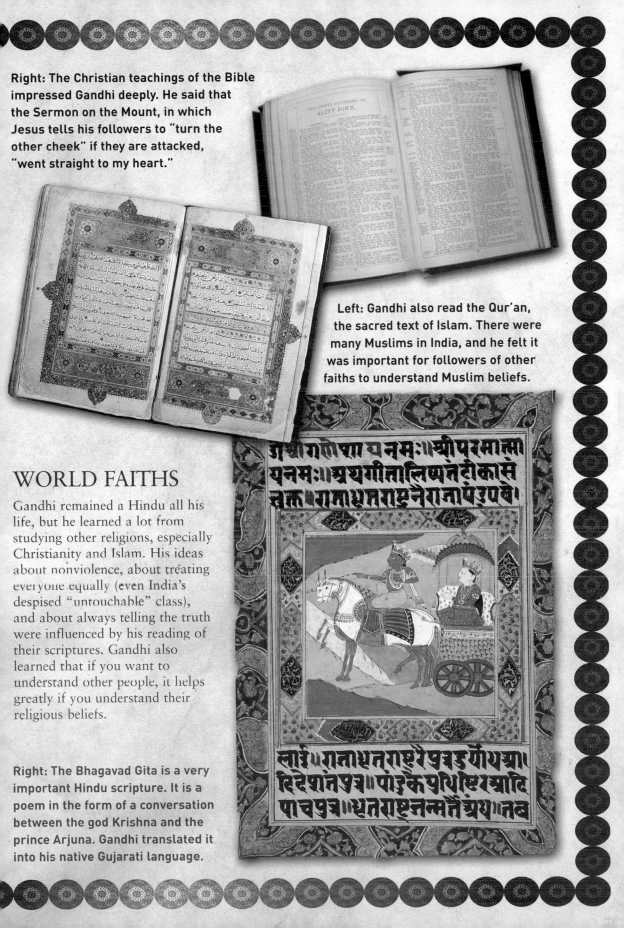

Right: The Christian teachings of the Bible impressed Gandhi deeply. He said that the Sermon on the Mount, in which Jesus tells his followers to "turn the other cheek" if they are attacked, "went straight to my heart."

Left: Gandhi also read the Qur'an, the sacred text of Islam. There were many Muslims in India, and he felt it was important for followers of other faiths to understand Muslim beliefs.

WORLD FAITHS

Gandhi remained a Hindu all his life, but he learned a lot from studying other religions, especially Christianity and Islam. His ideas about nonviolence, about treating everyone equally (even India's despised "untouchable" class), and about always telling the truth were influenced by his reading of their scriptures. Gandhi also learned that if you want to understand other people, it helps greatly if you understand their religious beliefs.

Right: The Bhagavad Gita is a very important Hindu scripture. It is a poem in the form of a conversation between the god Krishna and the prince Arjuna. Gandhi translated it into his native Gujarati language.

Traveling to South Africa

When Gandhi returned to India, things went badly. First of all, he learned that his mother had died while he was away. The news had been kept from him. Then he got a job as a lawyer but found it difficult. He was good at the written work but was too shy to stand up and speak in court. So, in 1893, when he heard of a job in South Africa, he jumped at the chance.

Below: Natal in South Africa had long been the scene of battle and bloodshed. The Zulu people had fought fiercely against Boer settlers, and later against the British, before finally being defeated in 1879.

In the 1890s, South Africa consisted of four states (the Orange Free State, the Transvaal, Natal, and Cape Colony), all ruled by white people, either the British or the Boers. Black Africans and Indian immigrants had few human rights. There were 75,000 Indians in South Africa. They had traveled there hoping for a better life than they could have in India.

1892
Gandhi and Kasturbai's second son, Manilal, is born.

1893–1894
Gandhi works as a legal adviser to Dada Abdullah, an Indian company with a branch in South Africa.

Many of them were indentured laborers or their descendants. In other words, they came to the country to do a particular job for a fixed number of years. Often they worked on British-owned tea, coffee, or sugar plantations. These laborers worked hard for low wages. After their terms had ended, the majority stayed on rather than make the long sea journey and restart their lives back in India. All Indians in South Africa were often attacked and harassed, and were not allowed to go out after dark.

Gandhi's first job in South Africa was in Pretoria as a legal adviser to an Indian company named Dada Abdullah. Soon he started hearing stories about how badly Indians were treated. Gandhi was himself thrown off a train for traveling in a first-class carriage, even though he had a first-class ticket.

Right: Indian street traders like this boy could make a decent living in South Africa, but they were treated very badly by the white ruling classes.

1894
Gandhi organizes the Natal Indian Congress to help the Indian community in South Africa.

June 1896
Gandhi returns to India for a while. He makes speeches explaining the problems faced by Indians in South Africa.

He felt he had to do something for South Africa's Indians. He called a meeting of Indians in Pretoria. His determination to help them win their human rights seemed to make his shyness disappear and he gave his first public speech with ease. He formed an Association of Indian Settlers so that all the Indian groups—Muslims, Hindus, and others—could come together.

After a year, Gandhi had completed his legal work with Dada Abdullah. But Indian traders in the Natal had heard about him and wanted him to stay on and help them. So he set up a law office in Durban in the Natal and soon had work fighting cases for the local Indians.

In 1896, he decided to return to India to bring back his wife and two sons to live with him. When he returned to South Africa, a group of white troublemakers attacked him. He was kicked and beaten, and people threw bricks and stones at him. The attackers knew he was going to campaign for the Indian people and did not want him to succeed.

Right: When Kasturbai came to South Africa in 1897, the family was still growing. By 1900, Gandhi and Kasturbai had four sons. The two youngest, Ramdas and Devdas, were born in South Africa.

1897
The Gandhi family arrives in South Africa. Gandhi and Kasturbai's third son, Ramdas, is born.

1900
Devdas, the Gandhis' fourth son, is born.

Left: When Gandhi (seated i his own law office in South A were soon busy taking on ca Indian people. Most lawyers were white and did not want Indian clients.

But attacks like this made Gandhi even more determined to help. He was soon busy writing to the newspapers and speaking at meetings. Gandhi knew that South Africa's rulers would be unwilling to make changes. But he fought to get Indians treated fairly in the courts.

Many of Gandhi's campaigns were overshadowed by war. In 1899, the Anglo-Boer War broke out between two groups of white settlers, the British and the Boers. During the conflict, Gandhi organized an Ambulance Corps to help the injured on the British side. Over 1,000 Indians served under Gandhi. They worked hard, got on well with the British troops, and saved many lives. When the British had defeated the Boers in 1902, they were thankful for Gandhi's work. But Indians were still being harassed. Gandhi founded a weekly journal, called *Indian Opinion,* which kept the Indian population informed. He began to campaign for Indian human rights once more.

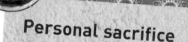

Personal sacrifice

When the Gandhis visited India in 1901, their friends gave them many farewell presents. Gandhi insisted that they should give these away to raise money for the campaign for the Natal Indians. Kasturbai even donated her gold jewelry.

1903
Gandhi opens a law office in Johannesburg.

1904
Gandhi founds the Phoenix Settlement, a community where he lived with Indian and European families.

Peaceful Protest

In spite of Gandhi's work, life remained tough for South Africa's Indians. In 1903, he moved to Transvaal, one of the four South African states, and set up a law office in Johannesburg. In 1906, the Transvaal government passed a law ordering Indians to register with the government and be given a registration certificate. They had to carry this with them at all times.

The law was just one example of the way Indians in the Transvaal were discriminated against. They had to pay a special tax, too. The government also refused to recognize marriages that were carried out in the traditional Hindu way. Gandhi invented a new form of protest, which he called *satyagraha*, a term that combines two words meaning "truth" and "force." The term meant that Indians would stand up against injustice and would carry out protests, but they would never do so violently.

Left: Gandhi (bottom right) sits with friends and his son Devdas (top right) outside a tent on Tolstoy Farm near Johannesburg. The farm was a country retreat where Gandhi and his fellow protesters lived.

1908
Gandhi is arrested and put in prison several times for his part in the satyagraha protests.

1910
South Africa becomes a united state, the Union of South Africa.

Left: Gandhi (front left) and a group of other satyagraha protesters line up outside prison just after their release in 1908.

Many Indians refused to register with the Transvaal government, and in 1908 some of them, including Gandhi, were thrown into prison for breaking the new law. While he was in prison, his guards took him to Pretoria to meet General Smuts, a leader of the Transvaal government. Smuts said he would abolish the law if the majority of Indians registered. But when Gandhi called off the protest and Indians started to register again, the government broke its promise. Soon, Indians were burning their registration certificates, and a full satyagraha campaign was underway.

Strikes began, and large groups of Indians defied the law by crossing from one state to another, something they were not allowed to do without permission. Finally, in 1914, the government gave in. They abandoned the special tax, agreed to recognize the Hindu marriage ceremony, and changed the registration law. At last, some justice had been achieved for Indians in South Africa. Gandhi felt that his work there was done. It was time for him to return to India.

Hard labor

When in prison, Gandhi spent nine hours every day at hard labor, breaking stones and helping to dig a water tank. The work exhausted him, but he did not faint in the heat as did some other prisoners.

1914
The government agrees to change its unfair laws.

1914
World War I begins.

RETURN TO INDIA

3

Settling Down

Gandhi returned to India in January 1915. He was given a hero's welcome because of his political work in South Africa. Many people expected him to enter Indian politics right away. But Gandhi had been away for most of the past 20 years, so he decided to learn as much as he could about what life was like in India.

Above: The writer and philosopher Rabindranath Tagore wrote many books, including poetry, novels, and plays. Gandhi met him soon after he returned home from South Africa.

Previous page: When he returned to India, Gandhi began once more to wear traditional local clothes, including a turban and sandals.

Gandhi was pleased to be back in India. He wore traditional Indian clothes and often spoke his native Gujarati language. As he traveled around India he met many interesting people. One of these was the writer Rabindranath Tagore, who had won the Nobel Prize for Literature in 1913. He saw that Gandhi's personality had an unusual, almost holy quality, and he gave him a new title, *Mahatma*, or "great soul."

During his travels, Gandhi met members of the nationalist movement. These were people who, like Gandhi, thought that India should be ruled by Indians, not by the British. But he was not yet sure how to bring about this change. He saw that in some ways the British governed fairly. He also respected their justice system.

January 9, 1915
Gandhi and his family arrive back in India.

May 1915
Gandhi founds his Satyagraha Ashram near Ahmedabad.

Left: On his travels, Gandhi (center) met many people in the Indian countryside. Most of them made their living by farming. They told him how hard life was for poor people all over the country.

And many of the British admired Gandhi. On his return to India the government gave him a medal for his medical services in the Anglo-Boer War.

Gandhi saw that life in India was difficult for many people, and would remain so even if India were ruled by Indians. He was especially sorry for the "untouchables," the people at the lowest level of Indian society. They had to do all the dirtiest jobs and had no education. Everyone else looked down on them, and many Hindus literally tried to avoid touching them.

Gandhi spent about a year touring India. Then he settled in western India, where he had started an *ashram*, or community, called the Satyagraha Ashram. Here Gandhi, his family, friends, and followers lived, grew food, and studied.

Right: Gandhi decided that he did not need a large, luxurious home like the one his parents had had in Rajkot. He, Kasturbai, and their children lived in this plain, simple house with very few comforts.

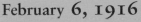

February 6, 1916
Gandhi makes a speech at Benares University. He criticizes the behavior both of Indians and their British rulers.

December 1916
Gandhi attends the Indian National Congress at Lucknow.

Solving Disputes

Gandhi's earliest political work in India was done to help the poor. But there was a problem at home. In 1915, Gandhi invited a family of untouchables to live in Satyagraha Ashram. Many members of the ashram objected and tried to get the untouchables thrown out. It looked as if the whole community might break up.

Below: When Gandhi began his campaigns for the untouchables, they usually had to live apart from everyone else. In the countryside they had to put up with the poorest housing and living conditions.

Eventually, Gandhi persuaded the others to accept the untouchables. But Gandhi's rich friends, who supported the ashram with gifts of money, pulled out. Gandhi was left without funds for his community. However, a wealthy businessman from nearby Ahmedabad, Ambalal Sarabhai, came to the rescue with a donation.

In 1917, Gandhi heard from a farmer in Champaran, in northeastern India. Like all landowners in this area, his British landlord had forced him to plant a crop called indigo, used for dyeing cloth. But the profits for indigo had collapsed, and the landlords were forcing the farmers to make up the losses with their own income. Gandhi decided to go to Champaran.

1917
The Montagu Declaration promises India eventual independence within the British Empire.

October 3, 1917
Gandhi secures a reduction in the amount the indigo farmers of Champaran pay to British landlords.

Right: These men are dyeing cloth, using natural plant-based dyes such as indigo. This craft had existed in India for centuries, and Gandhi realized the importance of supporting the country's indigo farmers and cloth-makers.

When he arrived, the British tried to force him to leave the area and local landlords insulted him. But these actions simply gave Gandhi more publicity. Soon the British government began an official inquiry into the question, and Gandhi was asked to take part. As a result, the government reduced the amount of money that the farmers had to pay.

It was not a total victory. The farmers still had to pay part of their income to the landlords, but their financial difficulties were much improved. Gandhi was pleased because the farmers had achieved their goal not with violence, but by using the legal system. Although the landlords had attacked many of the farmers, the farmers did not fight back. The campaign had shown that nonviolent action could work.

Gandhi's community

Gandhi's ashram contained everything necessary for a small community of people: a school, a farm with 150 acres of land, workshops, spinning equipment, and a large kitchen. It was like a small village.

1918

Gandhi begins to do his own cotton spinning, realizing that this is a useful and productive activity for Indians.

1918

Mahadev Desai, a young lawyer, becomes one of Gandhi's followers and his secretary.

Cloth and Spinning

Gandhi spent a great deal of time in his ashram spinning cotton fibers into thread on a simple hand-driven spinning-wheel. This might seem a strange activity for a man who devoted his life to campaigning for the future of his country. But for Gandhi, spinning was one of the most important things he could do. He wanted to show Indians how they could take control of an industry. Spinning was easy to learn—anyone could do it. If people produced their own thread, there would be no raw cotton for the British to export. Instead of being spun and woven in Britain, Indian cotton could be processed at home and Indian people would have the full benefit of their crop. The cloth could be used by the people who made it, or it could be sold in Indian markets, so that the profits would be kept at home. And Indians would not have to rely on the British to produce their fabric. Between 1942 and 1947 a spinning-wheel was shown on the Indian national flag, revealing the importance of spinning to the nation.

Below: Gandhi tried to spend an hour a day spinning and encouraged other Indians to do the same. He wore simple clothes—usually just a plain *dhoti*, or loincloth—made from cotton that had been grown, spun, and woven in India. Wherever Gandhi went, his dhoti reminded everyone of the importance of homespun cloth.

Right: Once the cotton was spun into thread, it was woven on a handloom to make *khadi*, or plain cloth. In the 1920s, encouraged by Gandhi, people all over India learned to spin and weave.

Below: Khadi was coarse and undyed, but Gandhi encouraged everyone to buy it to support the weavers. By doing so, people could show that they supported Indian independence.

From Protest to Tragedy

Even though he hated violence, Gandhi supported Britain in World War I. He was a loyal subject of the British Empire and thought that Britain might give Indians the right to rule their own country if they were loyal during the war. But although the government had promised reforms, it began to make life more difficult for those who objected to British rule.

Below: In Gandhi's time, farm work in India was done by hand, with either animals or human power used to pull plows and haul loads.

In 1918, the government devised a new law that imposed strict measures against those who wanted to protest British rule. The law was called the Rowlatt Bill and was named for Sir Sidney Rowlatt, the judge who headed the committee that drew up the proposed law. Under this bill, suspected troublemakers could be put into prison.

1918
The Rowlatt Committee issues its report, recommending extreme measures against suspected protesters.

January to March 1919
Gandhi travels around India making speeches against the Rowlatt proposals.

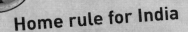

Home rule for India

The All-India Home Rule League was founded in 1915 by Gandhi's friend Annie Besant, a British woman then living in India. The League campaigned for Indian independence, and Gandhi joined it in 1920. Unlike Mrs. Besant, most British people in India did not support Indian home rule.

Trials could take place without a jury and without the right of appeal. A person could be imprisoned for two years for having an anti-government document. Rowlatt's committee believed that this would stop plots against British rule.

Many Indians objected and tried to persuade the British not to pass the new law. But the government would not listen: It looked as if the Bill would go ahead. Gandhi and other Indian leaders organized a protest throughout India. Gandhi's idea was to have a peaceful protest in the form of a *hartal*, a type of strike that also involves prayers and processions.

When the hartal took place in 1919, shops closed, no Indians went to work, and children did not go to school. The protest was largely peaceful, but Gandhi was arrested and held for a short time. After this, there were outbreaks of violence in some places. In Ahmedabad, public buildings were burned, and it was reported that several British people had been killed. Gandhi was upset: He had wanted a peaceful protest. But worse was to come.

Right: Many of the protests during the hartal were peaceful. People stopped work and joined demonstrations. This was the kind of protest that Gandhi had planned.

March 30, 1919
Protests and riots take place in Delhi.

April 6, 1919
Gandhi leads the hartal in Bombay (Mumbai) against the Rowlatt Bill.

At Amritsar in the Punjab, the hartal went peacefully until a procession was attacked by British troops, and Indians killed several British people in retaliation. As a result, the governor of the Punjab banned meetings and processions. But this did not stop a huge gathering of mainly Sikh protesters on a piece of land in Amritsar called Jallianwala Bagh.

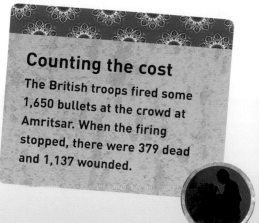

Counting the cost
The British troops fired some 1,650 bullets at the crowd at Amritsar. When the firing stopped, there were 379 dead and 1,137 wounded.

Jallianwala Bagh is a large square surrounded by buildings and walls. Around 20,000 protesters marched through the narrow entrance between two buildings into the square. Most of them did not know about the ban.

Below: Amritsar in the Punjab is the most important religious center of the Sikhs. The Golden Temple (left), with its roof covered with gold foil, is their most sacred shrine.

April 13, 1919
There is a massacre of Indian protesters by British troops at Amritsar.

July 1919 onward
Gandhi tours India, making speeches to explain that protests must be disciplined and nonviolent.

Above: The narrow entrance to the Jallianwala Bagh acted like a trap. Once there were thousands of people inside, it was impossible for most of them to get out quickly.

They were soon followed by British Brigadier-General Dyer with some 90 soldiers. Without warning, Dyer ordered his troops to fire on the protesters. Few of the Indians could escape from the square because the way out was so narrow. Hundreds of protesters lost their lives. As for the many wounded, Brigadier-General Dyer ordered that none of his men should help them in any way.

When Gandhi asked permission to visit the Punjab to see what had happened, he was refused. But he knew that a terrible tragedy had occurred, so he called off the hartal before further violence could take place. He felt partly to blame for the disaster and said that he had made a "Himalayan miscalculation"—an enormous mistake—in encouraging people to protest when they had not been properly trained in satyagraha.

One good thing had come out of the protest. The British realized how strongly Indians felt about British rule, so they finally decided not to accept Rowlatt's proposals. The massacre had one other important result: It showed Gandhi how ruthless the British could be in their effort to hold on to India. He realized that the Indian people would have to go through a long, hard struggle if they were to win the right to rule their own country.

October 1919

The government sets up a commission of inquiry into the massacre at Amritsar.

December 1919

The Government of India Act allows more Indians to vote and power-sharing between Indians and British in government.

THE STRUGGLE FOR
FREEDOM

In Prison

Above: After his illness and release from prison, Gandhi stayed at home, writing letters to his supporters and planning his future campaigns on behalf of the Indian people.

Previous page: This image of Gandhi as an old man became familiar worldwide as news spread of his campaigns for Indian independence.

In 1919 Gandhi became one of the leaders of the Indian National Congress. In 1920 he became president of the All-India Home Rule League. He began to draw together the different groups, of all religions, who wanted independence for India. They began a campaign against the British government. But once more, the campaign ran into trouble, and Gandhi found himself in prison.

Thousands joined Gandhi in "non-cooperation" with the British government. Some people gave up working for the British. Some sent back awards the British had given them. Others refused to buy cloth imported from Britain. Then a group in Gujarat refused to pay their taxes. But soon after this tax campaign had begun, violence broke out, and Gandhi stopped the protest. The authorities still arrested him for trying to destroy the government's authority. He was pleased at the sentence of four years that the court gave him: He welcomed the chance to think and do some reading.

With their leader imprisoned, the campaigners began to argue with each other. Hindus and Muslims wanted independence to work in different ways.

September 1920
The Indian National Congress agrees to the non-cooperation movement planned by Gandhi.

1922–1924
Gandhi is in prison for causing civil unrest.

They began to fight among themselves. Meanwhile, Gandhi became ill with appendicitis. This resulted in his being released from prison after only two years.

Once he was free, Gandhi decided to do something to bring Hindus and Muslims back together. He announced that he would go without food until the two sides reunited. Indians did not want Gandhi to starve to death, so his tactic worked. But after another year of political work, Gandhi decided to take a year off from politics. He hoped to give himself time to rest and to think about how best to campaign for self-rule. For most of 1926, he stayed at his ashram.

He realized that for life to improve in India it would not be enough to end British rule. Many of India's problems would have to be tackled. Untouchables were still despised by many, and there was great poverty. Gandhi would need to combine protest against Britain with real changes in the future.

"I ran the risk and if I was set free I would still do the same.... I am, therefore, here to submit not to a light penalty but to the highest penalty. I do not ask for mercy."

Mohandas Gandhi during his 1922 trial

1928
Gandhi leads a tax strike against the British all-white Simon Committee that examines India's constitution.

1929
The Indian National Congress announces that its goal is full independence for India.

The Salt March

In 1929, the British were still refusing to discuss Indian independence. So Gandhi planned a new kind of protest. He decided to break a hated law that gave the British government the sole right to gather and sell salt. In 1929, Gandhi marched to the coast. There he gathered his own salt from the seashore, in defiance of the British law. Many did not know what to make of this unusual protest, but Gandhi knew what he was doing. When people found out about the march, protests against British rule spread. People gathered salt, burned British cloth, and went on strike. Thousands of protesters, including Gandhi, were imprisoned. News of the march spread worldwide.

Below: Some 78 friends, fellow campaigners, and members of Gandhi's ashram joined the nationalist leader on the Salt March. Here he is shown walking with the poet and politician Sarojini Naidu (right), who was one of his most devoted supporters.

Satyagraha Ashram
Ahmedabad

Wasna

Anand

Mahl River Bank

Samni

Ankleshwar

Gulf of Camby

Delad

Right: The route of the Salt March stretched from Gandhi's ashram near Ahmedabad to the town of Dandi, 229 miles down the coast. The journey took Gandhi and his followers 24 days.

Dandi

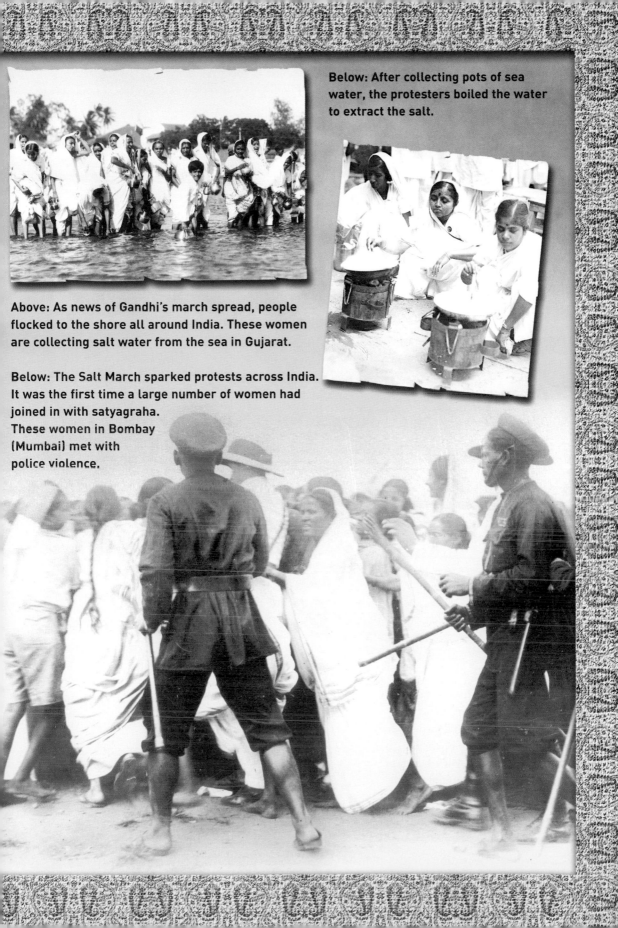

Below: After collecting pots of sea water, the protesters boiled the water to extract the salt.

Above: As news of Gandhi's march spread, people flocked to the shore all around India. These women are collecting salt water from the sea in Gujarat.

Below: The Salt March sparked protests across India. It was the first time a large number of women had joined in with satyagraha. These women in Bombay (Mumbai) met with police violence.

Quit India!

The Salt March was a success. The size and fame of the protest forced the British to release the protesters from prison and allow people to make their own salt. The British also allowed Gandhi to go to a conference in London about India's future. But the road toward full home rule was still to be long.

When Gandhi arrived in England in 1931, he was warmly welcomed. Ordinary people liked him, and he also met and charmed the famous, including royalty and the film star Charlie Chaplin. But the conference did not go well. Separate voting for untouchables was proposed by some of the other Indian delegates, but Gandhi thought that the untouchables should be treated just like other Hindus.

Back in India, Gandhi started another fast, this time to persuade the politicians to change their plans for the untouchables. He was successful. He spent the next few years doing welfare work for the untouchables and other poor Indians. He taught people how they could get a good, nourishing diet by growing and making foods themselves.

Above: The 1931 Round Table Conference proved difficult. The British and Indians disagreed about how India should be governed, and Gandhi had to cope with arguments among the Indian delegates.

September to December 1931

Gandhi visits London for the Round Table Conference on the future of India.

1935

The Government of India Act gives India limited home rule, with self-government for each province.

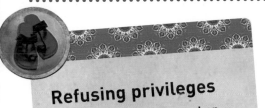

Refusing privileges

Unlike most prisoners, when Gandhi was in prison in 1942 he was allowed to send lots of letters and have many visitors. But he did not want all these privileges. He asked the authorities to reduce the cost of his food: He did not want elaborate meals, just food that was edible and clean.

Britain took a big step toward Indian home rule in the 1935 Government of India Act. This gave control of local affairs to elected provincial governments. Then in 1939, World War II started, and Britain felt that it had to defeat Germany and Japan before it could give India independence. In 1942, the British politician Sir Stafford Cripps arrived in India. He had a plan for an eventual independent "Indian Union." Each province of India could decide if it wanted to join. Gandhi saw that this could divide India, as Muslim areas would not want to join a union in which most areas were Hindu. Muslim leaders, such as Muhammad Ali Jinnah, even said they wanted a separate Muslim state.

The Indian National Congress turned down Cripps's proposals. It demanded that Britain "quit India" right away—if it did not, another campaign of satyagraha would begin. The British arrested Gandhi and other leaders for anti-British activities, but this unleashed a furious protest. British people were attacked and government buildings set on fire. It seemed as if Gandhi's hopes for India would never be realized.

Right: Gandhi hoped that Muhammad Ali Jinnah (left) would see the benefit of a united India, but the Muslim leader finally held out for a separate Islamic state.

August 8, 1942
The Indian National Congress passes its resolution telling the British to "quit India."

August 9, 1942
Gandhi and his wife Kasturbai are arrested and imprisoned in the Aga Khan Palace in Poona.

Setback and Sadness

After the call to "quit India," Gandhi was once more imprisoned for nearly two years. Upset by the violence breaking out all over India, he again began to fast, hoping to calm things down. But he could not prevent two great personal tragedies from taking place.

Gandhi was imprisoned alongside both his wife, Kasturbai, and his secretary, Mahadev Desai. Desai had been with Gandhi for 20 years. During this time he had become more than a secretary: He was a highly intelligent man with whom Gandhi discussed all his major decisions. He died suddenly a few days after his imprisonment. His death was a huge blow.

Kasturbai had been imprisoned for announcing that she would speak at a meeting that Gandhi could no longer attend due to his arrest. It was common for her to step in for her husband when he was in prison. But she had been ill for some years and had had several heart attacks. Being imprisoned made her health worse. In February 1944, she died in Gandhi's arms.

Right: Gandhi's secretary, Mahadev Desai, went everywhere with his leader. He was imprisoned with Gandhi when he died, serving him to the last.

August 15, 1942
Gandhi's secretary Mahadev Desai dies while imprisoned in the Aga Khan Palace with him.

February 22, 1944
Kasturbai Gandhi dies.

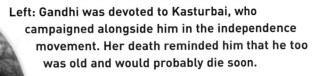

Left: Gandhi was devoted to Kasturbai, who campaigned alongside him in the independence movement. Her death reminded him that he too was old and would probably die soon.

They had been married for more than 60 years. Gandhi could not imagine life without her. His own health began to worsen. A few months after her death, the authorities decided to release him. It took Gandhi until autumn 1944 to recover and to restart his political work. He was convinced that it was important to make peace between Hindus and Muslims—even if this meant granting the Muslims their growing wish for a separate state. He and Jinnah met, but they could not come to an agreement over India's future.

But things were starting to change in Britain. World War II ended in May 1945, although Japan was not defeated until August, and the British elected a new government. A Labour prime minister, Clement Attlee, replaced the Conservative Winston Churchill, who had opposed Indian independence. The Labour Party quickly announced that they wanted India to be self-governed—and soon. There would be an election in India, followed by an assembly to draw up a new constitution. Change was coming at last.

Right: There were demonstrations after Gandhi's imprisonment in 1942. Many of these turned violent, and in Bombay (Mumbai), police used smoke to clear the crowd. Some people, overcome by the smoke, had to be carried to safety.

September 9, 1944
Gandhi begins talks with Muslim leader Muhammad Ali Jinnah.

1945
World War II ends. A Labour government comes to power in Britain and determines that India should be independent.

Death and Mourning

There were huge disagreements between followers of India's Hindu and Muslim religions about how the country should be run after independence. These disagreements led to rioting and bloodshed. Gandhi tried to calm things down, traveling around the country to try to stop the fighting. Meanwhile, the British tried to speed through the preparations for independence, hoping that this would also bring peace.

Above: Gandhi has tea with the new British representative, Lord Mountbatten, viceroy of India in the months before independence. Mountbatten praised Gandhi for trying to keep the peace between Hindus and Muslims.

India finally became independent on August 15, 1947, but only after a partition into two new countries. Alongside an independent India, a separate Muslim state, Pakistan, was formed. Pakistan was in two parts, West Pakistan and East Pakistan. These later became Pakistan and Bangladesh. Gandhi was sad that so many people had died during the struggle for independence and that there was still unrest, with Hindus and Muslims struggling for their rights.

Millions of people joyfully celebrated Independence Day, but Gandhi did not feel that he could join in the parties. Instead, he began another fast, which succeeded in its aim of bringing peace to the city of Calcutta (Kolkata).

March 22, 1947
Lord Mountbatten arrives in India. As viceroy he begins the process of making India independent.

August 15, 1947
Independence Day: India is now divided into two independent, self-governing, countries, India and Pakistan.

His final fast was a similar attempt to stop fighting in Delhi. But the violence carried on—and now some of it was directed toward Gandhi. Extremist Hindus thought he was too sympathetic toward the Muslims. One of these Hindus, Nathuram Godse, went to a prayer meeting attended by Gandhi. After bowing to Gandhi, Godse shot him. As Gandhi realized he was dying, he called to the Lord Rama, saying, "Hey Rama" ("Oh God").

Millions mourned for Gandhi. Jawaharlal Nehru, Gandhi's friend who had now become prime minister of India, paid a moving tribute to him (below). The great leader was given a traditional Hindu funeral, with his body burned on a funeral pyre.

> *"The light that shone in this country was no ordinary light... that light represented the living truth...drawing us from error, taking this ancient country to freedom."*
>
> **Jawaharlal Nehru on Gandhi's death, January 1948**

September 1, 1947
Gandhi begins a fast to try to end the violence between Hindus and Muslims.

January 30, 1948
An extremist Hindu, Nathuram Godse, assassinates Gandhi.

Gandhi's Achievements

Above: People celebrated in the streets on the first Independence Day, August 15, 1947, and Indians have celebrated on this day ever since.

Gandhi felt that his life had not been a success. He deeply regretted the violence and loss of life that happened during India's struggle for freedom and in the months just after independence. But today, historians believe that Gandhi was a successful and very important figure, both for his work in India and his influence all over the world.

Gandhi's work was hugely important in India. He made life better for many poor people, helping them to make a decent living. He also encouraged the production of local products, such as yarn and cloth. He helped many Indians understand that the untouchables are human beings who deserve rights just as much as the rest of the population.

September 11, 1948
The Muslim leader Muhammad Ali Jinnah dies.

January 26, 1950
The new Indian Constitution is adopted and India becomes a republic within the British Commonwealth.

And he showed people that they could prosper without the help of the British, who had controlled India for centuries.

His efforts aimed at gaining self-rule for India were significant. Without Gandhi, the terms for self-rule would probably have been less favorable, and the country might have had to wait much longer for independence. Although Gandhi was sad about the bloodshed, many more people would probably have died without his tireless efforts to make peace.

For people outside India, Gandhi is still an amazing example of what can be achieved without violence. Many countries ruled by an outside power have to go to war to win their freedom. But Gandhi showed that satyagraha is just as powerful a way to victory. He was the first political leader to use nonviolent protest in this way. Since his time, many leaders, such as Martin Luther King, Jr., who fought for the rights of black people in the United States, have been inspired by Gandhi's methods. Everyone who tries to change the world for the better using peaceful means owes something to Gandhi. Like Nehru, they can say, "Let us be worthy of him. Let us always be so."

Right: Pictures of Gandhi were carried at this meeting of the World Social Forum—a gathering to promote justice and wellbeing in society—in Mumbai (Bombay) in 2004. Wherever people meet to campaign peacefully for freedom, they remember "Mahatma" Gandhi.

1964
The Civil Rights Act is passed in the U.S., largely because of the nonviolent campaigns of Martin Luther King, Jr.

2005
India and Pakistan are still in dispute over control of Kashmir, a region on the border of the two countries.

Glossary

allegiance loyalty, usually to a government or ruler.

All-India Home Rule League organization devoted to campaigning for Indian independence and self-government.

ashram community, often living apart from the rest of society. Ashrams are usually led by a Hindu leader or holy man.

Boers Dutch (plus French) colonists who settled in South Africa in the 17th century, and their descendants.

castes the four main classes into which Hindu society is traditionally divided. A person is born into their caste, and so cannot move from one caste to another.

colonist person who settles in a distant land that is under the control of their native country.

Congress the Indian National Congress, India's most important political party. Congress was originally founded to enable Indians to discuss policy with the British. Later it campaigned for independence.

constitution document or law containing the basic principles that determine how a country is to be governed and setting down the key rights of its citizens.

dhoti simple loincloth of homespun cloth traditionally worn by men in India.

diwan prime minister or official who governed on behalf of an Indian prince.

empire group of countries or territories under the control of a single ruler or government.

fast to go without food. Fasting is often linked to religion, but Gandhi fasted to try to achieve political and social goals.

hartal traditional form of protest in India, which could involve prayers, processions, fasting, and not going to work.

Hinduism India's most ancient religion, still followed by millions of people in India and elsewhere. Followers of Hinduism are called Hindus.

home rule government of a state, city, or colony by its own people.

Indian National Congress *see* Congress.

indigo tropical plant that produces a violet-blue dye.

Inns of Court institutions in the city of London where people train to become barristers (lawyers who are qualified to plead cases in the higher courts).

Islam religion that teaches that there is one God and that Muhammad is his prophet. Islam has many followers in southern Asia, especially in Pakistan and Bangladesh. There are still many in India.

Jainism ancient Indian religion that forbids harm to any living creature.

khadi a plain, homespun cloth worn in India.

maharaja Indian prince or ruler of one of the ancient Indian states.

Mahatma title given to Hindus who show great holiness or wisdom. The literal meaning of the word is "great soul."

Muslim follower of Islam.

nationalist a person who loves his or her country and is especially loyal to it.

non-cooperation means of protest involving a refusal to work with the ruling government; for example, a refusal to pay taxes.

partition dividing something into several parts. This term was used to describe the division of India that created the separate nation of Pakistan.

prince local ruler of an Indian state under the British Raj.

pyre fire used to cremate a corpse at a traditional Hindu funeral.

Raj term used for the British rule of India.

Rama human form of Vishnu, one of the most important Hindu gods. Gentle and brave, Rama is greatly revered by Hindus.

Ramayana a long poem, written down about 2,000 years ago, which tells of the adventures of Rama and the kidnapping and rescue of his wife, Sita.

round-table conference meeting of different political parties or groups, at which each has the same rights during the discussions.

Sanskrit ancient Indian language in which the Hindu holy books and epic poems, such as the *Ramayana*, are written.

satyagraha form of nonviolent protest and resistance developed by Gandhi to campaign for the rights of Indians in South Africa and India.

Sikhism Indian religion with many followers in the Punjab region of northwestern India.

socialist a supporter of the system of government in which all industry and its profits are controlled by the workers.

strike to stop work as a form of protest.

Theosophist follower of Theosophy, a religious and philosophical movement that developed in the late 19th century. Theosophy tried to bring together the common threads in all religions.

turban man's headdress made by winding a length of cloth around the head. The turban is worn by most male Sikhs, and also by some Hindus and Muslims in India.

untouchable member of the lowest Hindu class—lower than all four of the castes (*see* castes). Untouchables were traditionally despised by other Indians. Even today, some still face prejudice.

vegetarian a person who does not eat meat, fish, or, in some cases, any food that comes from animals.

viceroy official who ruled India on behalf of the British monarch.

Bibliography

Books about Gandhi:

The Life and Death of Mahatma Gandhi, Payne, Robert, published by Bodley Head, 1969

The Life of Mahatma Gandhi, Fischer, Louis, published by Harper Collins, 1997

Mahatma Gandhi, Adams, Simon, published by Franklin Watts, 2002

Mahatma Gandhi: His Life and Influence, Kumar, Chandra, & Puri, Mohinder, published by Heinemann, 1982

M.K. Gandhi: An Autobiography, Gandhi, Mohandas, published by Penguin Books, 2001

Books about the history of India:

A Concise History of India, Watson, Francis, published by Thames & Hudson, 1974

A History of India, Stein, Burton, published by Blackwell, 1998

A History of India Volume 2, Spear, Percival, published by Penguin Books, 1965

The Lion and the Tiger: The Rise and Fall of the British Raj, Judd, Denis, published by Oxford University Press, 2004

Some websites that will help you explore Gandhi's life and the history of India:

www.mkgandhi.org
A website devoted to Gandhi, giving details of his life story.
www.mahatma.com
An in-depth look at the life and times of Gandhi.

www.indianchild.com/history_of_india.htm
Contains all kinds of information about India, including the struggle for independence, and about Gandhi himself.

Index

Acknowledgments

B = bottom, T = top, L = left, R = right.

Front cover Getty Images/Hulton Archive; **1** Corbis/© Bettmann; **3** TopFoto/Dinodia; **4T** TopFoto/Dinodia; **4B** Getty Images/Hulton Archive; **5T** Getty Images/Hulton Archive; **5B** Getty Images/Hulton Archive; **7** TopFoto/Dinodia; **8** TopFoto/Dinodia; **9** Getty Images/Hulton Archive; **10** The Bridgeman Art Library/Royal Asiatic Society, London; **11** The Bridgeman Art Library/Private Collection; **12** Scala, Florence/Philadelphia Museum of Art; **13** Scala, Florence/Public Record Office, London; **14T** Corbis/© Hulton-Deutsch Collection; **15T** The Bridgeman Art Library/Private Collection; **15B** Getty Images/Hulton Archive; **16** TopFoto/Dinodia; **18** Scala, Florence/HIP/British Library, London; **20** Scala, Florence/HIP/ British Library, London; **21** The Art Archive/British Library; **23** Getty Images/Hulton Archive; **24** TopFoto/Dinodia; **25** Getty Images/Hulton Archive; **26T** Scala, Florence/HIP/Ann Ronan; **26B** Getty Images/Hulton Archive; **27TL** The Bridgeman Art Library/Archives Charmet; **27TR** Private Collection; **27B** The Bridgeman Art Library/© The Trustees of the Chester Beatty Library, Dublin; **28** Corbis/© Tim Wright; **29** Getty Images/Hulton Archive; **30** TopFoto/Dinodia; **31** TopFoto/HIP/Jewish Chronicle Ltd; **32** Getty Images/Hulton Archive; **33** TopFoto/Dinodia; **35** Getty Images/Hulton Archive; **36** Getty Images/Hulton Archive; **37T** TopFoto/Dinodia; **37B** Getty Images/Time Life Pictures; **38** Getty Images/ Time Life Pictures; **39** The Bridgeman Art Library/Private Collection; **40–41** Getty Images/Hulton Archive; **40** Getty Images/Time Life Pictures; **41T** Getty Images/Time Life Pictures; **42** Corbis/© Scheufler Collection; **43** TopFoto/Dinodia; **44** Corbis/© Blaine Harrington III; **45** TopFoto/Dinodia; **47** Getty Images/ Hulton Archive; **48** Getty Images/Hulton Archive; **49** Corbis/© Bettmann; **50** Getty Images/Hulton Archive; **51TL** Corbis/© Bettmann; **51TR** Corbis/© Bettmann; **51B** TopFoto/Dinodia; **52** Getty Images/Hulton Archive; **53** TopFoto/Dinodia; **54** Getty Images/Time Life Pictures; **55T** Link/Dinodia; **55B** Getty Images/ Hulton Archive; **56** TopFoto/Dinodia; **57** TopFoto/Dinodia; **58** Getty Images/Hulton Archive; **59** Getty Images/Robert Elliott/AFP.